# ROSITA

# RSITA

Tom C. Patten
Robert Carpenter

Pacesetter Press
A Division of Gulf Publishing Company
Houston, Texas

To Dr. C.L. Kay, B.A., M.A., LL.D.,
of the Lubbock Christian
College, his wife Ruth, and their
four lovely daughters.

The rain clouds were approaching in formidable array as Tom Patten stood outside the terminal of the City of Durango's airport. Surely they will be on this one, he thought as another plane rolled awkwardly toward the terminal like a huge bird in a strange environment. He had been standing there for more than an hour watching the procession of commercial and private jets uncommon to a city which normally rested languidly like a dozing giant in the foothills of the Sierra Madre Mountains of northwest Mexico.

He was not alone in his vigil. Nearby was Leon de la Cruz, standing tall and debonair in his tailored dark suit trying to appear nonchalant. With him were his parents, Don Fernando de la Cruz, proud of demeanor befitting his title of the Silver King of Mexico, and his wife, Delores, a gracious lady of serene countenance. She was chatting with other members of the family.

"I've never seen so much traffic," he heard the English accent of a woman awaiting an outgoing plane, "What's going on?"

"There's a big wedding coming up," came the voice of her companion. "Some say it's the biggest in Mexico's history."

"Oh?" the English woman replied. "Who's the lucky bride?"

Her companion smiled and retorted, "Mexican aristocracy, you can bet on that."

Yes, Patten reflected, aristocracy of the most unusual kind and his eyes softened as he noticed Rosita stepping from a plane, followed by her stepparents, Dr. and Señora Yves Elluard, other members of the family, her governess and servants.

Leon was the first to greet them. He hastened forward and took Rosita's hand. He kissed it quickly with little display of emotion as is the custom. Following this, he leaned forward and bobbed his face affectionately close to one and then the other cheek of Señora Elluard before they patted each other on the back, a common greeting in Mexico. He followed the same ritual with Dr. Elluard.

Others moved in to welcome the arrivals and finally it was Patten's turn. He kissed her hand as she said with dancing eyes, "Señor Patten, how nice of you to be waiting."

"I've been waiting years for this," Patten replied with a choke in his voice. How lovely . . . how beautiful she was, he thought with affection, and such a wondrous blithe spirit, her voice tinkling like clear water rippling down a singing stream, her face an oval of perfection, her light brown cheeks flushed with excitement. Yes, he repeated to himself in adoration of this young lady of distinguished carriage and attire, she truly deserved her title of Miss Mexico and the right to become the wife of Leon de la Cruz.

Dr. and Señora Elluard were beside him now and they greeted him warmly. "We would have been here sooner but some luggage was misplaced," Yves Elluard apologized. "And such traffic." He chuckled. "It seems everyone is flying to Durango."

"Like a flock of geese," Patten replied. He turned toward Señora Elluard, a petite lady whose face was beaming as if in the rays of a rainbow, and said, "I'm happy for you."

"For all of us," Danelle Elluard said quietly. "For all of us."

Patten rode in the limousine reserved for Rosita and her stepparents, along with her *dueña*. Another limousine, containing Leon and his parents, followed as sedans trailed behind with friends and relatives. The protocol in Mexico is rigid indeed, Patten thought. Rosita had been chaperoned since childhood by her *dueña*, Consuelo, a Mexican woman with solemn features now seated in the front seat of the Mercedes with the chauffeur. At tonight's festivities, and during the two day wedding celebration, Consuelo would move like Rosita's shadow. She would play the same role then as she had throughout Rosita's life and courtship with Leon.

Soon it would be over, Consuelo thought as she gazed out the window of the car. Three days from now the lovely child who had matured into a lady would be separated from her forever. It brought tears to her eyes and she blinked them away. She loved Rosita as a mother loves a daughter and this was a triumphant moment for her beloved one. She should be happy, too, she reminded herself.

"I've reserved the entire top floor of the Casa Blanca Hotel for you and your guests," Patten was saying. "It's quite luxurious for Durango, but nothing like the elegant hotels in Mexico City. And remember, this is the city of scorpions."

"Yes, Yves has told me," Señora Elluard replied. She had never visited Durango and the threat of scorpions frightened her. "Is there danger even in the Casa Blanca?"

"I'm afraid so," Patten said. "I've found them in my suite. Be sure to instruct your servants . . . all garments on hangers. Nothing left on the floor day or night. You'll find wires dangling from ceilings. These are for shoes."

Señora Elluard shuddered. "Is their sting as deadly as they say?"

"A sting from the larger male ones is painful but not fatal," Patten said. "The grey females are the deadly ones. That's why the government has taken such extreme precautions. If a female penetrates the skin of a victim there's not much time. Only about thirty minutes unless serum is injected into the veins. There are public service treatment stations throughout the city with ambulances waiting.

"In the proper sections where there are no telephones, if someone is stung they rush to the street and shout, "Scorpio! Scorpio!" The alarm is relayed by others who hear the cry until the message reaches a treatment station."

How primitive, Señora Elluard thought and Patten sensed her reaction.

"This is the most primitive city in Mexico," he said. "The twentieth century has pretty much passed it by. Surprisingly, though, there are very few deaths and the natives have adopted a philosophical attitude. The local baseball team is called the Durango Scorpions and curio shops are stocked with scorpion mementoes of various kinds as a reminder of Durango." He smiled. "They've become a source of revenue for the children. They attach strands of white thread around captured scorpions and pit one against another in tournaments in the square, then solicit coins from spectators."

"How macabre," Señora Elluard said, wincing with the thought of the wedding being marred by a venomous sting. Hastily she changed the subject with a glance out the window. "So that's the famous iron mountain of Durango."

"Indeed it is," Patten said, and he grinned. "I guess I sound like a guide on a tourista bus, but it's truly a fantastic deposit of ore. It's a mile long, more than a third of a mile wide and its deposits contain an estimated 600 million tons of high grade ore worth hundreds of millions."

"Incredible," Señora Elluard said. "And the silver mines?"

"Mostly south of here in the Zacatecas region. A party of friars with their armed escorts was sent in 1558 into the mountains to convert Indians to the Catholic faith. They discovered an enormous paradise of silver. Other friars moved north into Durango and these cool and grassy uplands proved ideal for the raising of oxen and goats, descended from animals brought by Coronado. The Spaniards established ranches and slaughtered animals, not for their meat but for their hides and hoofs. But enough of that. The Casa Blanca is up ahead."

Rosita had remained silent during the drive until now. She spoke as she noticed several hundred persons lining the sidewalks and in the street. She said tremulously, "All those people. Surely they're not. . . ."

Patten interrupted with a chuckle, "Indeed they are, my dear. They're waiting to catch a glimpse of Señorita Rosita Elluard, Miss Mexico, and after the ceremony tomorrow you will be addressed as a Princess.

Rosita sighed. She would have preferred a less ostentatious wedding, and so would have Leon, but they were resigned to the strict requirements of marriages among the upper class of Mexico.

"We'll bear with it, my beautiful flower," Leon told her just before he returned to Durango. "And then?" His face brightened in anticipation. "Then we will be together forever as long as we live, and our lives will be one continuous song."

Three more days of waiting, she reflected, before they would fly in his father's jet to Mexico City for a brief pause before spanning the Atlantic to Spain for their honeymoon, and presentation to Spanish Royalty.

The limousine had pulled to a halt in front of the hotel now and there were ripples of applause and exclamation as she crossed the sidewalk and entered the hotel. The ornate lobby was crowded. As if in a trance she was introduced and heard her parents and Patten exchange greetings before she entered a waiting elevator.

Patten left them there, saying to Dr. Elluard, "The reception is at five o'clock. I'll be waiting in the lobby."

He went to his quarters where he carefully placed his clothes on hangers and hung his shoes from ceiling wires before taking a bath and stretching out on the bed. The Latin custom of siestas had its good points, he thought, as he closed his eyes.

The city of Durango is populated by a few enormously wealthy families of Spanish descent and approximately 100,000 Mexicans of Spanish and Indian blood whose income ranges from low to middle, with the poor comprising a majority of its citizens. The city's dwellings are mostly one-story adobe with inadequate sanitation and little or no modern conveniences.

The wealthy are proud of their ancestry and they zealously protect its purity. Their customs and marriage requirements are as rigid as those in the old country. If these customs are violated, the son or daughter is disinherited. They speak Castilian Spanish in contrast to the Mexican dialect and often there is a problem in communicating between the two classes. There are many other language barriers, because each of the many small Indian tribes in the untamed mountain areas has retained its own form of speech dating back many centuries.

The de la Cruz home is the showplace of Durango. Known respectfully as the "Palace," the two-story sandstone structure occupies a full block a short stroll from the cathedral, which is said to be the oldest in Mexico, and has a domed ceiling striped in gold and other trappings, which attest to the treasures claimed by the conquistadors after Cortez crushed the Aztec's rule under Montezuma.

The Palace has a fortress-like appearance with its immense carved doors and small barred windows. The heart of the mansion is a patio, approximately one-fourth the area of a football field, which is surrounded on all four sides by the open-topped structure. The patio is landscaped with native and imported shrubs, flowers and trees, gushing fountains, statuary and other ornaments. The house, itself, contains elaborate reception and dining rooms on the first floor, while some thirty bedrooms with private baths comprise the second floor. Overhanging balconies with roof and ornamental iron railings provide each suite with a view of the patio, upon which señoritas may look down and greet guests.

The antiques, paintings, hand carved furniture, tapestries and other works of art rival that of many museums.

Patten was waiting in the lobby shortly before five o'clock as Rosita and the Elluards stepped from the elevator. Patten fondly observed how stunning Rosita looked in a light blue gown, designed in Paris for this occasion. Señora Elluard was radiant also, in fetching white.

Others in the lobby, many dressed for the gala occasion, stepped aside as Rosita and Señora Elluard proceeded to their waiting limousine. The chauffeur opened the door amid admiring murmurs from townspeople gathered for a glimpse.

Leon welcomed them at the great entrance door. He was joined by his parents and they were ushered inside as four string bands in various parts of the patio began playing in unison, "Mexicalli Rose," the most beautiful rose in Mexico.

It was a stirring moment for Patten and he recalled poignantly how he had gazed from the street at the immense structure when he first arrived in Durango more than fifteen years ago in his search for the Lost Mines of El Diablo. He had regretted at the time he lacked the credentials to take a peek inside the Palace under the guidance of Don Fernando, knowing full well this was an impossible dream since he was an unknown Americano—an intruder in the eyes of Mexican royalty.

And now I am here, Patten thought. It had taken many years, but here he was.

He was acquainted with only a few of the hundreds of guests, but he was introduced to others and they chatted convivially in Spanish. Some of them asked politely about his mining ventures, and he in turn, expressed interest in their various endeavors, but the main topic was the marriage of such an attractive bride of noble birth and the handsome groom who bore the name, de la Cruz. Among those he knew was Jesus Sanchez, a mining engineer and a brother of Señora de la Cruz who recently had visited his tin mine at El Diablo. Sanchez, florid of face and ebullient, led him to a table where an enormous silver bowl was surrounded by silver goblets.

"This is a happy moment for me," Sanchez said as they accepted champagne from servants dressed in colorful Mexican costumes. He blinked his eyes emotionally and continued, "Leon has always been my favorite. Almost like a son. My only regret is I have no sons, but if God had willed, I would want them to be like Leon. And Rosita!" He gazed toward her. She was standing beside her future husband chatting with guests. "She is without a doubt the most charming, the most poised young lady I have ever met. They will have many children and the de la Cruz heritage will flourish through the centuries." He touched Patten's arm and said, "Come let us look at the wedding gifts."

The presents, placed on a long mahogany table, one-fourth the length of the patio, represented a horde of diamond and emerald rings, fine linens, paintings, statuary, and gold and silver works of art along with silverware, china, goblets and such an assortment of unusual objects that Patten was reminded of a fabulous auction he had attended in London years ago.

"It pays to get married," Sanchez chuckled. "Especially if you're a de la Cruz."

Indeed it does, Patten thought, Rosita would live like a princess the rest of her life.

The hours went by with the champagne and music creating a festive mood and a buffet of delicacies on long tables covered with exquisite lace tablecloths, typical of cosmopolitans accustomed to gourmet foods.

Finally it was time to leave. Patten joined the Elluards and Rosita. After bidding Don Fernando and Señora de la Cruz good evening they left the Palace, with Leon saying adios on the steps with a look of anticipation. "Tomorrow morning," he said softly to Rosita.

"Yes, my love," she replied, "Tomorrow morning."

Rosita settled back in the car, thinking with satisfaction, tomorrow at nine o'clock she would be by the side of Leon, facing the priest in the cathedral filled to capacity by invited guests, and after the ceremony she would be the bride of the man who had courted and claimed her heart.

Although Rosita slept restlessly, she felt refreshed when awakened at 6 o'clock, and she chatted happily with Consuelo and her attendants as she ate a light breakfast in her room. Rosita had begun grooming when Señora Elluard entered and directed the preparatory activities. Rosita's white satin wedding gown, with silver weave and tiny pearls, was slipped over her head and smoothed. Finally she was ready. She gazed at her reflection in a full-length mirror and adjusted her diamond and emerald encrusted tiara.

"Do I look all right?" she asked, and Señora Elluard beamed her approval.

The reception was at eight o'clock in the palace and precisely an hour later the bells of the cathedral began their joyous peeling. Rosita had been waiting for their sound, and so had Leon, standing beside her in his dark silk suit. Taking her hand, they led the procession from the house, as townspeople across the street burst into applause. It was indeed a princely promenade to the cathedral a block away. Don Fernando had placed silver blocks in double rows in the middle of the street for them to walk upon. After the ceremony, the blocks would be sent to Rome as a gift to the Catholic church in commemoration of the wedding, but now they echoed with the footsteps of the soon to be bride and groom.

Leading the couple was the priest in his regal robes, and gold cross dangling from his neck to his waist on a heavy gold chain. Behind him were Leon and Rosita followed by their families with many others trailing until the line extended from the palace to the cathedral. It appeared to Rosita, as she kept in step with Leon, that the entire city had gathered for the occasion and it seemed that way to Patten, too, as he gazed at the thousands overflowing into the street and in front of the church. The bells in the tower of the cathedral were peeling out beautiful chimes in the sunny, crisp morning air. They seemed to be tolling out their love for the future happiness of beautiful Rosita.

The bride's parents and relatives sat in the front rows of the church on one side of the center aisle while his family occupied the front rows on the opposite side. In the rear were the flower girls, ready to follow the bride and groom down the aisle.

Rosita stood stiffly, nervous now, with her attendants adjusting her bridal gown in her dressing room in the rear of the church, while Leon and his attendants waited expectantly on the other side. Guests flowed like an almost unending stream into other rows until the cathedral was filled and the organ swelled with inspiring music.

As Patten entered and found his seat, he breathed a prayer of thanks. Life had been good to him, he thought, and now Rosita's was being fulfilled as he had never anticipated.

Rosita and Leon walked upon blocks of silver on their way to the cathedral.

The bride and groom were moving to the rear center aisle now, where they stood awaiting the flower girls to assemble. Then they walked slowly down the aisle.

The group halted in front of the altar and the sonorous voice of the priest rolled through the church with Latin utterances unfamiliar to Patten. Dr. Elluard stepped forward to give the bride away to Leon and the ceremony began.

It would last more than two hours, Patten had been informed, and would be entirely in Latin, but the time or the language was of no consequence to him. Rosita, whom he loved so much, had achieved the impossible.

As the priest continued a ceremony virtually unchanged since the birth of the Catholic Church, a faint smile spread across Patten's face. He was one of three persons among the hundreds in this great cathedral who knew the secret of Rosita and how this talented, sophisticated young beauty as a child was a blind, starving savage abandoned with her dying mother by their Yaqui tribe in the fierce wilds of the Sierra Madre Mountains.

*As the couple knelt at the altar, Patten's thoughts faded into the past and the secret of Rosita.*

A plane was landing. It was an OX-5 Jenny with a ninety horsepower motor. The year was 1917 and the United States was at war with Germany. From the frail aircraft stepped young Tom Patten, his face flushed with pride in much the same manner Rosita's would be many years later. Patten had just completed his first solo flight with the fledgling U.S. Air Force at Rich Field in Waco, Texas, thus assuring himself, he felt certain, of an overseas assignment with other members of his squadron.

"Well done, Tom," his flight instructor told him as he walked toward the hanger.

"Thank you, sir," he replied.

It was a moment he would never forget, but his desire to go overseas was denied when it became known to his commanding officer that he was only seventeen, not twenty-one.

After being discharged because of his youth, Patten returned to school. During the next several years, he attended Texas A&M, the University of Texas and Vanderbilt University where he majored in engineering and law.

During the summer months, he earned money for the next school term working as a stunt pilot with Gates Flying Circus. He performed daredevil feats at county and state fairs and offered rides for bolder spectators eager to experience the thrill of flying through the air in the strange contraptions. On one occasion, Patten flew under the Brazos River bridge at Waco, Texas, a clearance of sixty-feet, much to the concern of his family and thousands of persons lining the banks.

Patten purchased his first plane when the Air Force announced the sale of surplus crated planes of World War I vintage in Americus, Georgia. He acquired a new 90 HP - OX 5 for $590. The sale attracted scores of young aviators, many of whom had seen combat in Europe. Among those he met was a young lanky, soft-spoken pilot by the name of Charles Lindbergh, who a few years later would become an international hero as the first aviator to make a solo flight across the Atlantic. Patten mentioned that he had been rejected by the Air Force and Lindbergh confided to him that he, too, had been rejected, with his instructor saying he was totally unqualified for flying.

The 1920s were good ones for Patten and he saved some money during the immediate years after college. He became interested in oil exploration and his first efforts were in the Brown County fields west of Fort Worth. He brought in some shallow wells which produced a scant five or six barrels a day, but it was a start and his appetite was whetted. He then began drilling in the Breckenridge field and it was there that a friend came over to his drill site and said, "Hey, Tom, that old fool finally came in with a "discovery."

"All wildcatters are fools," Patten grumbled. "Which one are you talking about?"

"Dad Joiner."

"Yeah. You mean the old man finally proved the major's wrong?"

"He sure did. He brought in a gusher on the Daisy Bradford farm."

Patten, as all persons in the oil industry, either personally knew or had heard of Dad Joiner. Then seventy years of age, Joiner had endured years of ridicule in his search for petroleum in East Texas. Despite innumerable failures, he had persisted in his belief that an ocean of oil lay beneath the wooded farmlands. Several exploratory wells had been drilled by the major oil companies in this same area. They had been dry and the larger companies had forsaken the region for productive ones in other parts of Texas and elsewhere.

Joiner's faith had remained steadfast. He managed, somehow, to raise sufficient moneys from local people or oil men in Houston and Dallas. These wells, too, were dry, but Joiner never lost hope.

Even in the depression year of 1930 he kept drilling and his discovery well on the Bradford farm in October led to the development of the largest oil field on the North American continent. It covered more than 140,000 acres and over the decades would produce more than 2 billion barrels of crude.

This was a golden opportunity, Patten decided, after hearing of the Joiner discovery. He knew that the majors had few acres under lease. It would be a matter of getting there fast.

He was not alone with this thought. Within weeks the depression-ridden town of Kilgore increased in population from 700 to 10,000 and other nearby communities experienced similar growing pains. As stated by James A. Clark and Michel T. Halbouty in their authoritative book, *The Last Boom,* it became, "The most frenzied oil boom in the nation's history. It was the California gold rush, the Klondike, the Oklahoma land rush and the wildest of all past oil booms rolled into one."

Patten hastily drove to Tyler, some twenty-five miles from the Joiner well, where he stayed with the family of Col. J.H. Herndon, a friend of his father's. Other wells were being drilled now and lease hounds were knocking on dilapidated farm house doors with offers of wealth if land-owners would sell their leases.

Patten decided that London, an unincorporated village of some 100 persons, was an ideal place to drill, but when he arrived a friend told him the majors had gotten there first.

"There's not a lease left, except maybe the streets," his friend remarked with a smile.

Why not drill in the streets? Patten asked himself.

He talked to the more prominent citizens in the small town and arranged for London to be incorporated. Then he leased the streets, paying $27,000, payable out of one-fourth the oil, for a total of one and three-fourths acres.

His bold maneuver brought much resentment and a vigilante committee was formed. One night, they carted away the timber he had bought for construction of a derrick. Undaunted, Patten hired a former Texas ranger, Clyde Yancey, widely known as a rugged, hard man, to stand guard as a new derrick was constructed and drilling began.

When the well came in, Patten removed the derrick, sank telephone poles on four corners of a twenty foot square around the "christmas tree," and constructed a one room house over the flowing well. It became known as a penthouse over a gusher as publicized in Ripley's *Believe It Or Not,* and in newspapers throughout the world. To townspeople and oil men in East Texas, it was known as the "Tower of London on Alibi Hill." Patten drilled two other producers in the middle of the main street, all averaging more than 10,000 barrels of oil daily, and he was the first to bring in producers inside the city limits of London, followed by the first flowing producer in Kilgore on the J.A. Knowles Tract.

After the rigors of World War II, Patten directed his attention toward Mexico and from that moment the

*Patten's penthouse, built on top of an oil gusher, was publicized in Ripley's* Believe It or Not.

bizarre role he was to play in the life of Rosita began to develop, although it would be years before they met.

Patten had visited Mexico on several occasions as a tourista. As a mining engineer, he was aware that vast hidden treasures of gold and silver, and virtually every mineral known to man, still remained locked in its formidable mountains, despite widespread small mining operations which began after Cortez invaded Mexico in 1519 and shattered Montezuma's Aztec empire. Galleons loaded with gold and silver made Spain the richest and most powerful nation in the world until England and France challenged her rule. Centuries later, hundreds of mines were in operation and new ones were being discovered.

Patten was fascinated with stories of legendary lost mines; mines located in remote areas with wily prospectors coming into villages using nuggets to purchase supplies and then backtracking along narrow trails to elude those seeking the location of their motherlodes. Some of these prospectors left the country with their fortunes. Others died of natural causes. Many were slain by Indians hostile to outsiders who dared invade their domains. There were reports that Indians, often unaware of the worth of gold and silver, had killed the prospectors and then covered mine entrances with earth to prevent others from defiling their land. There were other tales by lone survivors telling of the massacre of their comrades after they had found rich lodes in regions controlled by hostile Indians.

There are isolated areas in Mexico still under the control of Indians who live as primitively as centuries ago. The most formidable is the Yaqui nation in the southwestern part of the state of Chihuahua and the state of Sonora which extends westward to the Gulf of California and northward to Arizona. There is an imaginary line some sixty miles north of Durango which marks the southernmost boundary of their empire.

The conquistadors attempted to subdue the Yaquis in their conquest of Mexico, but they failed, as did the Mexican government when independence was achieved centuries later. Although Yaqui villages near the borders were overrun and placed under Mexican control, the towering barriers of tangled mountains and barancas, or gorges, that cut thousands of feet into the bowels of the earth have protected the Yaquis. It is suicidal for a *yori* (white man) or a Mexican to enter. It is said that when a Yaqui child cries he is warned by his mother, "Be quiet or the *yori* will get you," and when the child is older, "The *yori* killed your father, your grandfather and my mother. Son, kill the *yori*. Never trust a *yori*." It is their boast they are *la raza de bronce que sabe morir*, (The bronze race that knows how to die) and they have been, and remain, the most tenacious defenders of their virgin land, of anyone in the world. Perhaps this is why their northern cousins the Apaches, so fiercely resisted "the white devils."

There is gold in the Yaqui nation. J. Frank Dobie, a colorful raconteur and scholar of the Southwest, relates in one of his books of a Yaqui chief crossing into Arizona in 1892 with a buckskin sack of gold nuggets and telling James B. Gray, chief of scouts on an Apache reservation, "We trust you. Buy guns and ammunition for us with this."

Gray sold the gold and bought two hundred and fifty U.S. Army rifles and half a million rounds of ammunition in New York. Marked "Agricultural Implements" the crates were shipped by boat to Galveston and by wagon to Tucson. The weapons were clandestinely carried across the border by Yaqui runners and resulted in the Indians trapping a regiment of Mexican soldiers and annihilating them—one of many such instances in their efforts to remain free, with gold providing their means of remaining well armed through the generations.

As Patten made plans to visit Mexico, this time hunting for lost mines or perhaps investing in proven ones, he had no idea his travels would take him into the heart of the Yaqui empire, under their watchful but protective eyes, to become one of the few white men who has viewed their riches and been permitted to return to the outside world.

"Let's drive down to Mexico," Patten suggested to Jack Winters, the son of a petroleum engineer in Houston. "I'll pay the expenses and you do most of the driving."

"Sounds good to me," Winters replied. He was a student at Texas Christian University in Fort Worth and the summer months lay ahead. "Anything particular in mind?"

"I thought I would look around. Talk to some people. Possibly invest one way or another."

It was a leisurely trip to Laredo and across the Rio Grande into Mexico. They paused in Valles and took rooms in a venerable hotel. After bathing and changing clothes, they strolled down an avenue to a popular cafe. Seated nearby were several Mexicans. They were drinking and their voices were loud. Patten listened, bored at first but then intrigued. He soon realized they were talking about lost mines and in particular the lost mines of El Diablo. They were saying this was the most fabulous of all the lost mines; that it had provided Cortez with immense troves of silver and gold before it had been abandoned. The men speculated the Indians had wiped out the Spanish force and concealed the entrance to the mine.

One of the men scoffed, "They've been looking for El Diablo like the lost island of Atlantis. It's just a lot of loco talk."

"Maybe, maybe not," another said. "But I know from experience. I have been in those mountains west of Durango and they all deserve the name of El Diablo. It truly belongs to the devil."

"If it's there, it's not in Yaqui country," another said.

"True enough. Not even Cortez could get there."

"It's located west of Durango," another voice spoke, "But it will never be found. Like Montezuma's buried treasure, it's gone . . . gone . . . gone forever."

Patten was intrigued. Arriving in Mexico City, he went to the departmental office where donouncements of claims are recorded: a denouncement meaning to survey and lay legal claim to mineral rights. Once filed, the prospector must pay taxes on the claim. If he defaults, he loses his rights and the title once again is returned to the government.

Patten leafed through hundreds of musty pages which recorded the triumphs, but mostly the tragedies, of mining operations. For every successful one, there were scores of failures and he wondered if it might be better to return to this familiar field in his own country.

At last he found mention of El Diablo. There was nothing specific, except to relate that the mines had been a major source of wealth in the sixteenth century and were believed to be located in Durango.

Leaving Winters to enjoy Mexico City, Patten took a plane to Durango. The lusterless city offered no appeal to him, but as he looked out a window from his suite in the Casa Blanca Hotel he could see the Iron Mountain and to the west a hazy outline of the towering Sierra Madres which, he sensed, contained an incredible wealth of concealed minerals. And, he told himself with a grimace, "The lost mines of El Diablo."

Patten found the Casa Blanca to be a cosmopolitan hotel and a headquarters for persons of many nationalities drawn there as investors, operators, specialists or suppliers in the mining industry. He met many of them. They were acquainted with the El Diablo legend but were engaged in proven operations. They had neither the time nor money to search for an elusive mine.

During the next few years when he could spare a few weeks from his drilling activities in the United States, Patten made several expeditions into the Sierra Madres, traveling in his plane to outlying airports, then by jeep and finally by foot with natives leading the way along tortuous trails sometimes too narrow for burros to turn around. He around. He located several abandoned lead and silver mines, none of which were worth re-working. But no El Diablo. It was out there somewhere, Patten kept telling himself, but where?

A major lead developed when he met an old man named Juan Raminez in a village west of Durango. The wrinkles in Juan's face were deep and his skin was as dry as parchment. He talked slowly as though each word might be the last one he would utter.

"There was an Americano many years ago who would come through this village with his pack train on the way to Durango for supplies," the old man said. "It was when I was a boy." He laughed dryly. "Mucho years ago. He hired me to take care of the burros and load the supplies in Durango and I know this to be the truth. He bought mucho months of supplies and paid in gold, the gold sometimes was the size of marbles. I don't know, but it may have come from El Diablo. No one went beyond this village with him. He disappeared into the wilds and although some from this village and others from Durango tried to follow, he was too smart for them. It is my belief he befriended the Yaquis in some way and they accepted him as a blood brother."

"Do you remember his name?" Patten asked.

The old man entered his adobe house and returned with a scrap of paper. "W. Tomas Moore," he said. "He said if I ever wandered into Yaqui country and needed help to tell them I was his friend."

Subsequently, Patten talked to an Indian chief in the village of Val Verde. The chief confirmed Raminez's story of Moore and said he believed the Americano left Mexico during the revolution and settled in San Antonio.

Patten checked court records in San Antonio which showed that a W. Tomas Moore died in 1948 at the age of 82. He had been married to a Mexican woman in the Village of Laxlam, now dead, who had given birth to three children, Thomas Jr., Alec and Carmen, whereabouts unknown, and Patten began to wonder if W. Tomas Moore was indeed, a loco Americano.

His spirits were revived when he met Paul Wilkinson, chief engineer of the famed Tayoltita mine, which had been owned and operated by the Hearst family since the beginning of the twentieth century when Senator George Hearst of California, wealthy beyond most person's conception from his Homestake Mine in the Black Hills of South Dakota, became interested in the abandoned mine.

Wilkinson invited him to visit Tayoltita and as they flew from Durango, he told Patten of its history.

"The Spaniards began production in 1600," he said, "and produced immense quantities of gold and silver for a long time. The metal bars were transported by burro caravans from Northern Durango until the sandstone trails were worn ankle deep to the coast.

"When they finally reached a bottom barren zone, they abandoned the mine, although a priest wrote his bishop in Guadalajara that during his visit to the Shrine of Guadalupe an image had appeared with a message during a religious ceremony, telling him there was a larger deposit of much richer ore than they had encountered in the upper areas and not to abandon the mine.

"Hearst was informed of the prediction as recited in old annals of the church and being an aggressive individual with ample funds to gamble, sent one of his geologists to examine the structure in Tayoltita. The geologist reported he could find no evidence from his sampling.

"Still not satisfied, Hearst sent his hard-rock superintendent, Captain Rawlins, who found a similarity to the Homestake Mine and expressed the opinion there was likely a large ore body below the 250-foot level.

"An exploratory shaft was sunk through the barren area and a vast deposit of high grade ore was discovered."

Wilkinson continued, "The story is told of the senator climbing a rugged mountain on foot, attired in spats, striped trousers, a fancy waistcoat, and covered by the flowing tails of a black Prince Albert to be defined by awed natives as the senator."

Wilkinson went on to relate, "The senator was justly proud of his son, William Randolph Hearst, who later founded the *San Francisco Examiner* and then a publishing empire which still exists. After electricity had been installed at the mine, the senator sent his son down to Mazatlan to inspect the Tayoltita mine. Captain Rawlings had prepared an elaborate feast with all the trimmings to welcome young Hearst, whom he knew. When the caravan approached, the captain stood on a ledge and waved his welcome but his elation was deflated when he found the young man was not in the caravan.

"The guide explained he had put Hearst on his best mule, but as they began to climb the second mountain he refused to continue the four-day trip over the rugged trail. From that time on, the captain and mine workers referred to William Randolph Hearst as 'Willy'.

When the company plane landed, Wilkinson took Patten on a tour of the mine and Patten was flabbergasted. Stacked in a pile were more than a hundred gold bars, each weighing thirty-two kilos, or 32,000 grams. At that time the value of Mexican gold was $1.05 in U.S. currency per gram.

*Each of these 120 gold bars is worth $33,600, making the total value of the pile $4,000,000.*

Patten was informed that each month the gold was transported by armored truck to the mine's air field where twin-engined planes flew it through the mountain passes to Mexico City, with natives keeping track of the day of the month by the flight of "the golden express."

Tayoltita, he was told, is operated by the San Luis Mining Company, with its field office in Mazatlan, Sinaloa, Mexico, and its main offices in San Francisco. It has been owned by the Hearst Estate since 1907, even during the Pancho Villa revolution, which, Wilkinson said, attested to the dominant personality of Senator George Hearst.

Inspired by the thought, if others can do it, so can I, Patten continued making trips to Durango, and on one he met Lionel Rydings, formerly a professor of geology at the University of Oklahoma. Rydings had been living in Mexico for many years and spoke several Indian dialects as well as flawless Spanish. He was interested in the folklore of lost mines and they became good friends.

"You've heard of the Lost Dutchman Mine, I suppose," Rydings said one day.

Patten nodded. It probably was the most glamorized of all lost mines and several books had been written, including some by Dobie, who as most writers, placed the location of the Lost Dutchman Mine somewhere in the Superstition Mountains in Arizona.

"I have reason to believe it's in Yaqui territory bordering Arizona," Rydings said. "Actually, it's not an original thought. There are several cheap paperback books in Mexico City dealing with lost mines and some of them show it to be there. The Yaquis have a fortune in gold but use it sparingly since their needs are modest."

Rydings told how they sent young braves over the mountains to Culiacan on the shores of the Gulf of California for supplies.

"They never walk, those Yaquis," Rydings said. "They trot down the street in Culiacan wearing nothing but head-bands and loin cloths and local people give them the right of way, you can bet on that. They're magnificent specimens. Tall for Indians, lean and muscular with light bronze skin unlike most tribes. They get their supplies mostly from the Sears store and they pay in raw gold. The manager totals their purchases and pretends to weigh the nuggets." Rydings chuckled. "He's the richest man in Culiacan."

Rydings said the Yaquis also have another source of income; opium, which they market but do not use.

"Their drug is peyote, the so-called diabolic root which they use in their primitive rites," Rydings said. "The first poppy seeds were brought by Hans Schmidt, the Dutchman, or at least that's what I've heard. Schmidt fell out of favor with German authorities and fled to America. Eventually he became a blood brother of the Yaquis under unknown circumstances. The poppy is still extensively grown there. The opium is rolled into large sticky balls, wrapped in banana leaves, and taken by runners over the mountains where it's sold to dealers and eventually smuggled into the United States."

Rydings said Schmidt, before fleeing Germany, left a gold medallion, similar to the one he wore, for his son, with instructions for him to come to America when he matured.

"Somehow or other the father got word to his son he was living in northwest Mexico with the Yaquis," Rydings continued. "He said the medallion would identify him when he arrived. Well, young Schmidt finally made it to America and across the continent to Sonora, but his father was dead. He told hostile Indians his father was Hans Schmidt and showed them the medallion. They exhumed the body

and sure enough the medallions were identical. I understand he's been living with them ever since."

"I'd like to visit that country and talk with Schmidt,"
Patten said. "He might have some information about El
Diablo."

Rydings paused before saying, "There's only one possible way and it's a long shot."

"I'm listening," Patten said.

"If we could get word to the Yaquis we had an important
message to give Schmidt, they might let us in. I don't
know, but I'd give my eyeteeth to take a look at that country."

Patten agreed to finance an expedition if Rydings could
work out details.

"Fair enough," Rydings said, "I'll head for Mexico City
as a first step."

"Why Mexico City?"

"I have some friends with the government's aviation
branch. They might be willing to drop some Yaqui
paratroopers in there and make arrangements for our
visit. That's about the only way to communicate with
them. If you sent emissaries along those trails they'd be
knocked off like clay pigeons."

Patten was aware that every young man in Mexico must
serve two years in the military service unless his family
had sufficient money to pay another young man to serve
for him. He was not aware that Yaquis also served, and
Rydings explained, "Only those who live on the outer edges
of the Yaqui nation are under Mexican control. But in the
interior," he laughed. "You can bet they aren't."

Patten was in his Houston office several months later
when Rydings phoned from Mexico City. "We've got
clearance," he told him. "I've just gotten word from the
Yaquis we can talk to Schmidt but we can't take anything
in or out. When can you make it?"

"Right away," Patten said. "Where should we meet?"

"Culiacan," Rydings said. "From there we can catch a bush plane to a Yaqui outpost and get instructions. Bring some good boots. It's going to be a long, hard walk."

The outpost, Patten found when he stepped from the small plane with Rydings, was a Yaqui village on a mesa bordering the mountains. They had purchased supplies in Culiacan, so they loaded them on burros and got set for the trek.

Their Yaqui guide told them it would be a five-day journey and said one of the dangers would be giant blood-sucking vampire bats. He told Rydings, with Rydings translating for Patten, there was a place with cliffs and deep-seated caverns which were infested with millions of them.

"We will stand guard at night to protect our burros and ourselves," the guide said.

Questioned further, the guide explained, "They're blood-suckers and if you're not careful you'll wake up in the morning and find your animals dead with all the blood drained from them. They have been known to attack a sleeping man covered in a sleeping bag. I'll tell you, Señor Rydings, it is not a pleasant thought."

"No," Rydings said, and Patten agreed.

They left the outpost and soon were in runt hills capped with red *topueste* dirt and as they ascended, they came to rocky terrain so rough and barren that only thorns grew on scrubby brush.

Finally they were in the mountains and their guide led them through passes that twisted tortuously and Patten could understand how invading armies of Spaniards and Mexicans had been wiped out. They saw no one but had an uneasy feeling they were being watched. When mentioning this to their guide, he shrugged and said, "Is this not the way it should be?"

On occasion their route took them through timbered mesas of pine, spruce and the red-hued *madronos* and lower into humid valleys with their lush vegetation and clear streams. There had been buzzards circling overhead in their walk through barren areas but now there were song birds and deer looking curiously at them.

"From one extreme to the other," Rydings remarked, "I think it was Milton who said there is a hell and a heaven on earth."

They trudged upward again. Toward dusk they stopped near a spring. It was a campsite identified by the ashes of many fires. It was chilly now and they were hungry. A fire was soon blazing and they warmed themselves as they prepared a meal. The guide pointed downward toward some caves in sandstone cliffs. "The vampire bats will fly from them at dusk," he said, "We will keep the fire burning bright."

The sun already had dipped below the mountains and soon from dozens of caves in the canyon below emerged swarms of bats, vibrating the air with eerie beeps. It was an awesome, fearful scene as if from Dante's *Inferno*.

"We are fairly safe up here," the guide assured them. "But we must keep the fires burning and keep watch all night."

After an uneasy sleep, they continued their journey and found several dead bats along the way. Some had wing spans of three feet and were loathsome in appearance with sharp pointed beaks and small piercing eyes. Evidently, their built-in sonar had been of little use in avoiding collisions with each other or some object.

"Are there any more bats along this route?" Rydings asked.

"Only back there, señor."

"Once is enough," Rydings replied.

In mid-afternoon they entered a Yaqui village with its primitive thatched huts and winding trails. The chief greeted them solemnly and spoke to the guide, who told

Rydings, "They have consented, but you must leave your guns and cameras here. You'll get them back when you return."

Rydings and Patten were disappointed. They had hoped to photograph the Lost Dutchman Mine if indeed, they saw it, and without their weapons they no longer felt secure against predatory animals.

They declined to spend the night in the village, knowing it was forbidden for foreigners to stare into the eyes of women or children. This was considered a bad omen, the evil eye, and if a Yaqui became ill the foreigner was held responsible. Playing it safe, they kept their eyes lowered, with only flickering glances at their surroundings.

"The custom dates back to the Aztecs," Rydings explained. "If anyone looked into the eyes of Montezuma, he was executed."

They traveled for another three days over more hospitable terrain and at last they came to a village of several hundred persons and the guide told them, "You will find Señor Schmidt here."

Schmidt had been informed of their coming. He stepped forward with the chief and extended his hand. Patten judged his age as about seventy. He was attired in a breechcloth with guaraches, or sandals. His skin was as bronze as an Indian. His eyes were blue and his long hair was white.

They were surprised when he spoke English, "Welcome. Why have you come?

"To talk to you. To offer you a return to Germany if you wish to come with us," Rydings said.

Schmidt smiled. "I would not know the country. I left there in 1910. I have heard we lost a war."

"Two of them," Rydings said.

The old man sighed. "One or two, it makes no difference." He waved his thin arms and his voice crackled, "Men have died fighting wars and I have lived in peace among my adopted people. And yet," he paused and ran his fingers through his hair. "It might be good to return, if only for a short time." He rubbed his eyes. "Sometimes I dream of the old country . . . the beer, the sausage and pumpernickel, the polkas . . . a world so different from this one and yet this is my home." He smiled proudly. "My father and I have created a new species of Yaquis. You will notice many with blue eyes and light hair. I love them all, but enough of that. You are my guest, my first guests over all these years who talk of my native country losing two wars. When were they fought?"

"The first one began in 1914 and lasted four years," Rydings said.

Schmidt bit down on his lip. "So long! how terrible! The casualties must have been heavy . . . my friends and relatives . . . it is a shame."

They were silent for a moment and then Schmidt asked, "And the second war, was it as bloody? When did it happen?"

"It began in 1939."

Schmidt frowned. "The years have been lost," he said. "What year is this?"

"It is 1949."

The shoulders of the German Yaqui sagged and his voice groaned, "That makes me older than I care to accept." He reached over and touched Patten's shoulder. "Yes, I think I would like to return to Germany. When should we go?"

"In a few days," Patten said, and he added, "You speak English quite well."

Schmidt smiled. "I studied it in school as a child and when I arrived in America I worked as a clerk in the Bowery of New York until I had money to travel. I haven't spoken it since then, but it comes back. Do either of you speak German?"

"No," they said in unison.

"It is a shame. I hope when I return they will understand me. It would be heartbreaking if they laughed."

The three men talked late into the night and Patten questioned him about the lost mines of El Diablo, with Schmidt saying he had never heard of them but that his Yaqui comrades had many mines in their domain.

"Including the Lost Dutchman? The one your father discovered?" Rydings asked.

"I do not know their names," Schmidt replied. "I only know they are rich beyond imagination."

They spent three days in the village and found it peaceful and prosperous, with an abundance of manufactured products their runners had carried from Culiacan and other cities. This included glass bottles with rubber nipples used to feed the infants warm goat's milk, aluminum pots and pans, silverware, plastic combs and brushes and just about everything, Patten remarked to Rydings, "except electric lawn mowers and after-shave lotion."

They were permitted one visit to a mine which they believed might be the Lost Dutchman, and found it to be literally a mountain of gold, with nuggets like pebbles in streams and exposed veins of gold ore glistening in the sunlight.

"I have never seen such a fabulous motherlode," Patten said, and Rydings agreed.

Patten managed to slip one nugget of some four ounces underneath his arm pit and carry it out of the Yaqui nation, knowing full well it might have cost him his life but wanting a memento of Yaqui treasure.

They were well fed on goat meat, called *cabrito*, venison, tortillas, roasted corn and bowls of hot barley mush with sugar cane. But in spite of Schmidt's hospitality, they spent a restless night. They were assigned a circular hut with a thatched roof. Their beds, which were in the middle of the hut, had been hewed from trees, like canoes, and had deer skins for cover and padding. About twenty feet away, a dozen braves circled them silently, never shifting their feet or batting an eye, as Patten and Rydings attempted to sleep.

Schmidt told them proudly of the way venison was provided. Instead of hunting them with firearms or bows, they were chased and caught by fleet-footed maidens who, it appeared, were major providers in many ways. The two Americans went with Schmidt one morning to a river with water twenty feet deep, but so clear they could see gravel on the bottom. The girls climbed tall, dead trees on the bank and sat motionless with knives in their mouths until they saw large trout meandering upstream against a mild current. Then they dived into the cold water like streaks of lightning and inevitably came up with their prize.

They witnessed a wedding ceremony between different tribes. It is the custom of the Yaquis, Schmidt explained, to separate their children from their parents at an early age. The boys are sent to one tribe and the girls to another. Marriage arrangements are made by their parents, with the bride and groom not meeting until the ceremony.

On this occasion, Patten observed the tribes met in their bark canoes at a fork in the river, with an exchange of presents and provisions for the couple, feasting began and would continue for two days. According to Schmidt, the newlyweds would bid farewell and move downstream in their canoe, pulling three or four others behind, loaded with their gifts, to start a new life at a clearing to their liking, never to return to their original tribes.

"It's primitive and perhaps brutal, but effective," Schmidt said. "If my country had had Yaqui braves in their ranks, my country, not yours, would have won both wars."

"Perhaps," Rydings said. "But now comes a time to leave. Do you want to come with us?"

"I think so," Schmidt said. "I think so."

The old man was strangely silent as they penetrated the mountain passes and spent another night above the canyon of the bats. When they arrived at the last Yaqui outpost he turned and said, "My friends, I thank you, but I do not belong in the world outside. It has been too long. I am returning home."

It probably was a wise decision, Patten and Rydings agreed. The transition probably would have been too much.

Later, in Durango, Patten casually mentioned he had visited Yaqui territory and may have seen the Lost Dutchman Mine.

They stared at him skeptically and said no white man entered Yaqui country and came out alive. He let it got at that.

Patten's efforts to locate the children of W. Tomas Moore succeeded at last when he received a letter from the director of police in Mexico City stating that W. Tomas Moore, Jr., was chief geologist of the San Francisco mines some 350 miles south of Durango. Elated, Patten flew there and took a jeep from the gravel landing strip to the silver mine. Moore, a sturdy, handsome man of about forty-five, greeted him warmly and listened attentively as Patten told him of his efforts to locate the lost mines of El Diablo.

"How did you hear of my father?" Moore asked.

Patten told him of Raminez and the Indian chief in the village of Val Verde who had said he thought Moore had gone to San Antonio.

"I checked the records in San Antonio," Patten said, "then started hunting for you, your brother Alec, and your sister Carmen."

"Carmen is married to Dr. Paul Adams who lives in Zacatecas," Moore said. "My brother lives in Yucatan, I believe, although we haven't corresponded in years."

Moore went on to say his father fled Mexico with his wife and children during an outbreak of violence when he was about eight years old.

"I remember crawling through narrow passages of a mine," he told Patten. "When I was older and living in San

Antonio he would talk about the mine but his memory had failed and his directions didn't make sense." He sighed. "I've looked for it too, many times, but finally gave up and got a job.

Moore said his father had a modest amount of money when he settled in San Antonio. He purchased a house in the Mexican section and put his three children through college; both sons graduating with mining engineering degrees and Carmen in liberal arts.

"After mother died, he lived alone on funds I sent him," Moore stated. "As a matter of fact I'm still paying taxes on the old place but it's uninhabitable. My vacation's coming up in a few weeks and I plan on going back. I might be able to sell the lot for a few hundred dollars. Anything would be better than paying taxes on near worthless property."

"Do you think he may have left a map or a description of the mine?" Patten asked.

"I don't think so, but there were some boxes stored in the attic. I went through some of them years ago and couldn't find anything but it might be worth another try, unless the mice have gotten to them."

"Would you mind if I went along? Patten asked. "If we could find something worthwhile I'd be glad to finance an expedition and you could have a share in the profits, if there are any."

This was fine with Moore.

They met in San Antonio, with Moore and his wife, Dr. Paul Adams and Carmen.

"When my brother wrote, I couldn't resist returning to the old place," Mrs. Adams said. "It's been so many years and there may be some family mementos; old photos and things like that worth keeping."

The house was indeed in ruins, with its windowpanes broken and the front door hanging on one hinge. There was not a piece of furniture left and plumbing fixtures in the kitchen and bathroom had been removed by scavengers.

They moved cautiously up the rickety stairs and walked down a hallway to a porch with shredded screens.

"This is where papa used to sit and rock," Carmen said sadly. "It was a fine old chair, handcarved in Mexico. I should have come and gotten it, but. . . . " She frowned. "Time slipped by."

Before leaving their hotel rooms the men had changed to work clothes and the women had changed to slacks and blouses with scarves over their heads as protection against dust. Moore had brought two Coleman lanterns and a ladder.

"That's the way up," he said, pointing toward a square panel on the high ceiling above. "It's possible our scavengers overlooked it or couldn't make it up. Anyway, we'll know in a minute."

He leaned the ladder against a wall and managed to lift the heavy lid. Crawling inside, he looked down and said, "It's hot as the devil and stinky but the floor's sturdy. Come on up and bring the lanterns."

With light, they could see several boxes, along with some suitcases, a trunk, lamps, chairs, an early model Victrola and stacks of records and books. They seemed fairly well preserved, indicating the roof did not leak and rodents had not invaded.

The women were assigned the dilapidated trunk and suitcases but they found little worth keeping among the musty garments, quilts, shoes and other personal items belonging mostly to Mrs. Moore, except in one purse Carmen dipped her fingers inside and squealed in delight when she removed a handful of nuggets.

"Look!" she shouted. "It's gold, real gold!"

"It's all of that," Moore said. "Four or five ounces. Mother probably put it away for a rainy day and then forgot about it. Keep looking."

Patten and the other men were going through the boxes. They found letters, which they read hopefully, worn prospector's clothes, an old Aztec stone time table. But finally, after hours of searching, Patten was leafing through a 1936 issue of *The Saturday Evening Post* when he found a manila envelope. He removed a tattered piece of paper and stared at the boldly scrawled words, "El Diablo." Beneath the words was a crudely drawn map with compass point directions.

"Come over here," he said to the others. His voice was calm but his heartbeat had quickened. Was it possible? He asked himself. Was this indeed a map to the lost mines or was it a fraudulent map like those peddled to gullible touristas in curio shops?

Both Moore and Dr. Adams examined the paper.

"It looks genuine to me," Dr. Adams said with a tremor. "But then. . . ."

"It's in dad's handwriting," Moore said.

Patten asked him, "Do you think your father may have drawn it when he was . . . , well, after his memory had failed?"

"I don't know," Moore replied. "But these compass point directions look pretty professional. I've a hunch, a strong hunch, it's genuine. I definitely think we ought to check it out."

Patten and Moore arrived in Durango with two engineers and the discolored map which they hoped would unveil a treasure stemming from Cortez. They absorbed the usual banter as loco Americanos who would never cease looking for El Diablo, but they remained smugly silent, not identifying Moore as the son of the legendary prospector who a half-century ago had purchased supplies with gold from his secret mine.

They assembled a caravan and followed directions on the map along trails for five days until they came to the base of a steep 9,000-foot mesa.

"This should be El Diablo," Moore said. His campanions studied the map and their compasses and agreed.

Tired as they were, they made it to the top of the mesa before nightfall. Although it was summer, a gale force wind was blowing and it was near freezing. Never did a place seem so cold. They fully understood why it was named the land of the devil!

After supper and a night's rest, they traversed the rugged terrain with its giant boulders and centuries old pine and oak trees. They found nothing to indicate mining operations of past generations or that man had ever seen the desolate spot.

"But of course," Moore speculated. "Any number of things could have happened. A growth of vegetation, the entrance sealed and covered by Indians, a land-slide . . . even an earthquake."

On the following day, the engineers finally agreed after painstaking survey work that, if the map was authentic the mine entrance was in a five hundred foot square area, 200 feet below the top of the mesa.

They covered the area foot by foot and could find no indication of past mining operations. It was a gamble now and Patten was calling the shots. It was his money and this had become a dice game. He was reminded of Dad Joiner, who kept gambling and finally won in East Texas, and of the Hearst's fabulous Tayoltita mine.

"If there's a mine shaft, it's buried," Moore voiced the opinion of everyone. Then, turning toward Patten, he added, "If you want to spend the money we can go back to Durango and get enough dynamite to blow the top off this side of the mesa."

Patten hesitated but then said, "Let's go." He told himself as they departed, this was his last effort to find El Diablo. It was now or never.

It took weeks to work. They brought in laborers and equipment and drilled three foot holes in a pattern for the dynamite, using more than three miles of electric line.

Once completed, they moved all camp equipment and animals across the canyon to a safe location, and watched the costly show. Patten's trembling hand pushed the plunger down and the whole top side of the mesa suddenly disintegrated, hurling huge boulders to the canyon floor thousands of feet below. The explosion thundered into their ears and blackened the sky with towering clouds of smoke and debris. They witnessed the devastation through binoculars, and as the air cleared, they began shouting and pointing, for in distinct view was a mine shaft which appeared to be chiseled from solid rock.

Hastily they ascended the mesa and rushed toward the shaft. They proceeded several hundred feet to other

*If the map was authentic, the mine entrance was not far away.*

tunnels which honeycombed the entire mountain and found skeletons and crude mining equipment used centuries ago but they found no trace of gold or silver ore.

"It's a tin mine," Moore said, and the others agreed. "High grade, though," he added as if to ease their disappointment. Tin had been used by the Aztecs and Spanish to blend with copper and make bronze. The Indians used bronze for arrow and spear tips and for carving tools. Cortez, after his conquest, was in need of artillery and scores of bronze artillery pieces were cast.

Moore would never know how the El Diablo map had come into his father's possession. He could only speculate that he had copied it from an original document, believing, as others, that the mine was rich in gold and silver ore.

Their disappointment was short lived, however, for the old map had led them to the largest deposit of tin ore on the North American continent with veins extending half a mile in length and within three feet of the surface. Tests showed the veins to run from 15.18 percent tin concentrate per ton to as high as 61.77 percent. Pure tin was worth $1.21 a pound on the market, and with an estimated reserve of more than a million tons of high grade ore in the mine, Patten and Moore had cause for celebration.

After a legal denouncement was filed in Moore's name, because he was a Mexican citizen, Patten returned to Houston, where investor acquaintances quickly joined him in forming a Mexican corporation with ample funds for mining operations. Moore was placed in charge of operations and Dr. Adams agreed to serve as company physician, working from his office in Zacatecas, where he was representing other mining corporations.

It was months before roads and an air field could be constructed, thus delaying the arrival of equipment needed for modern mining operations. Also delayed were plans to truck the concentrates from the mine mill to a railhead some twenty-two miles away, and then to the coastal port

*Because the market value for tin was $1.21 per pound, Tom Patten kept his pistol handy as a deterent against would-be banditos.*

of Tampico where it would be shipped to Texas City, Texas.

Finally the first convoy left El Diablo. It was met half way by twenty-five mounted banditos and the foreman in charge was given a message to relay to Señor Patten. Each truck leaving the mine would either pay 300 pesos as bounty, or be destroyed. The foreman in charge said the leader of the band tapped his rifle for emphasis.

Informed, Patten flew to Durango and talked to the governor.

The governor was friendly. "You are paying taxes and you have provided work for our people," he told him. "I will see that you are protected."

"It will take a company of troops," Patten suggested.

The governor wagged his finger and chuckled, "No, Señor Patten, not that many." He spoke to an aide and within moments two men entered. They were the largest Mexicans Patten had ever seen. He estimated their height as six feet two inches and their weight as 210 pounds. They were armed and their stolid features and calculating dark eyes gave every indication they were killers.

The governor said, "I think you will be amply protected by these two men, Señor Patten."

As they returned to El Diablo in Patten's plane they told Patten their names were Pedro and Manuel. Pedro, the leader, had seventeen notches on his pistol grip and Patten would learn later that he had long ago grown tired of cutting notches. He was the fastest gun in Mexico.

Pedro asked a few questions about the banditos and closed his eyes as if satisfied. Manuel already was dozing.

Despite their formidable appearance, Patten was uneasy. Another convoy would be leaving in a few days and he had no desire to risk the lives of his employees and the possible destruction of his trucks. He expressed his fears to Moore, who shrugged and said, "Those two hombres are the most feared gunmen in Mexico. Give them time."

*The governor of Durango said that Patten's mining operation would be amply protected by these two men, Pedro and Manuel.*

Mañana, mañana, Patten fretted. Why was it always tomorrow in this strange land? Why were not things done today? He smiled as he recalled an incident which occurred when he first had visited Durango. He had been scheduled to meet a train at noon, but a talkative native friend said, "There's no hurry, Señor Patten, trains never run on time in Mexico. Wait an hour or two."

Patten insisted on leaving. His friend accompanied him to the station, still protesting his haste. They arrived there shortly before noon and the train pulled to a halt at the station platform a few moments later.

"You were wrong, weren't you?" Patten scolded his friend, who replied, "But Señor Patten, that's yesterday's train."

And now, Patten continued to fret, it was mañana from Pedro and Manuel. He decided to delay convoy movement until they took some action.

Then one night as Patten was working in his office, Pedro knocked on the door and entered. Two six-shooters were holstered on his hips and a Browning automatic rifle slung over his shoulder.

"I am going to have a talk with the banditos," Pedro said. "I'll be back before siesta."

"You're not taking Manuel?"

"No need," Pedro replied with a grunt. "No need."

"There must be twenty or thirty . . . maybe more."

"No need, Señor Patten."

Patten watched him from the window as Pedro mounted his horse and jogged away under the light of a full moon. He'll be killed, Patten thought. No one, not even Pedro could handle that many armed banditos.

The night was cold and Pedro gave his horse free rein as he traveled along the winding road toward a village some twelve miles away. He hummed softly, for this was the kind of assignment he enjoyed. Born in Mexico City of impoverished parents, he soon had established himself as someone to be feared. Two older boys waylaid him in a dark street for the few pesos he had earned washing dishes in a cafe. He was eleven years old, but big for his age. And though his assailants were in their teens, he knocked one unconscious and the other fled.

A few years later he was hired as a chauffeur and bodyguard for a wealthy family. He served his two years in the army and won medals as a marksman. Later, he wandered from one gunslinging job to another. He had been wounded twice and he had learned to kill. It was his way of life. The governor of Durango had hired him four years ago as his personal bodyguard and he had no complaints.

Pedro had not been idle during his days at El Diablo. He had sent out scouts and they had returned with information of where the banditos lived and the name of their leader, Crispin. Crispin, he knew as a coward. He had been the one to flee that night many years ago in Mexico City. It will be a pleasure, he told himself, as he rode. Crispin deserved another lesson, perhaps a final one.

Pedro arrived in the village shortly before dawn. He watered his horse at a stream, stretched out on the bank, and had a smoke. At dawn he rode slowly along the streets until he came to the adobe house on the outskirts with fine horses in a corral, which he had been told was their hideout.

Pedro, never one to use a key for opening doors, hurled himself against the thick wood and smashed his way through, the automatic rifle in his hand. There was no need to fire. The men, who had been sleeping, were very much awake now. He pointed his weapon toward Crispin and said. "I did not come down from El Diablo to kill you, although it would be a pleasure. I am working for Señor Patten and this is my word: leave before sundown and never come back or I will kill you all."

He elevated his rifle and fired a volley into the adobe walls over their crouched bodies before departing. The banditos were a threat no more.

She had been born in darkness and darkness was familiar to her. She could hear the voices, smell the environment, taste the food she ate, feel the warmth of the sun and hear the whistle of the wind, but she could not comprehend sight. Existence for her was reaching out with her frail hands and touching her mother, or sitting on a stone and absorbing the movements and voices about her.

She was not aware that others could see, that she was handicapped. That is, she was not completely aware until alone with her mother on the mesa.

"Why are we here?" she asked. "Why did they leave us?"

"We were left to die," her mother said softly. "The others have gone."

"Why were we left to die and what is dying?" she asked.

"Dying," came her mother's solemn voice, "is leaving the mountains and the valleys and going to a happy place in the sky."

The child considered this for a moment and asked, "They didn't want us with them any more?"

"We could not take care of ourselves. In this world it is necessary." Her mother coughed. "I do not breathe well. My body aches. I cannot walk fast. And you." She stroked her frail face with her rough hands. "You are blind."

"What is that?"

"You cannot see."

"What is that?" the child persisted.

"It means you cannot walk the narrow paths without being led. It means you cannot pick the berries when they are ripe. It means you cannot see the trees and the flowers and the birds. It means you must depend on someone else to help you."

"But I can feel the trees," she said. She turned and ran her fingers over the rough bark of a pine tree. "It feels so big. How tall is it? Does it touch the sky? When we die do we climb the tree into the place of happiness?"

"No, my child," her mother replied in a tired voice. "The tree does not touch the sky. The sky is beyond the stars that shine at night. The sky is farther even than the moon that glows when the sun goes down on the other side of the mountains."

"I can feel the sun," she said.

"Yes, you can feel the warmth of the sun."

"What is the sun like?"

"It is hot and fiery and it moves from the east to the west and this is called daylight. After it sails across the sky it is what is called night. This is when we sleep for the night can be treacherous with its wild beasts who hunt for food and sometimes will attack a person in their hunger. This is why at night we gather close to each other with our fires to light the darkness and protect us."

"I have touched fire," said the little girl.

"Yes, I remember."

"It hurt."

"Fire is not to be touched. It is like the sun, hot and fiery and a servant to our needs but it must be handled carefully, otherwise it will strike back in anger."

"I can feel the sun so it is daylight."

The woman coughed. "Yes, it is daylight."

"I can hear the birds. They sound happy and we are not, my mother. Why are the birds happy when we are not?"

"You are asking questions I cannot answer."

The child began to whimper. "I wish we could leave," she said. "It is lonely here."

"There is no place to go, my daughter." She handed her a piece of venison jerky and a mango. "It is time to eat. Then we will go to the spring to drink and bathe our bodies."

The child ate slowly and then spoke, "You said there were *yoris* near here?"

"Yes. On the mesa on the other side of the canyon."

"Why are *yoris* so evil?"

"That is the way they are," the woman spoke in hate. "They come from distant lands to destroy what is ours, what has been ours long before I was born, long before my parents and their parents and others even before them."

"Why do they want to destroy?"

"I don't know. It is the way they are and you are making me tired with so many questions. You are like a sparrow that never stops chirping."

The child's voice quivered. "I do not want to die. I want to live."

"Come, let us go to the spring," her mother said.

"There's been some movement over there," Pedro told Patten. He pointed across the canyon to another mesa of smaller elevation. Last night I noticed a campfire. I wonder if Crispin or some of his gang decided to stay."

"We've had no trouble with our convoys," Patten reminded him.

"Not yet," Pedro growled, "But I think we ought to take a look."

They formed two parties, each of six armed men, one to follow a trail down to the canyon and upward on the west side of the mesa, the other on the east.

It was arduous, but hours later Patten and his group were on the east side of the mesa and he presumed Pedro's unit had arrived on the west. The mesa was smaller than El Diablo and scantly wooded. They moved cautiously, fearing an ambush. It was an ideal place, Patten warned himself, and he wondered if this was Crispin's way of retaliating against Pedro's brash threat. He crouched, startled, when he heard a scream somewhere ahead. It was a shrill, hysterical cry and it was followed by others.

Pushing forward, they came to Pedro and his men. They were grappling with a frail Indian woman who was screaming her fears in a dialect he could not understand. Squirming in the arms of another man was a child. Her

They were grappling with a frail Indian woman and a small child.

wails were piteous but the face of the man was bleeding from her clawing fingernails.

"Tie their arms and legs but don't hurt them," Pedro shouted above the clamor. He could kill men with no regret but he had no desire to harm a woman and child, no matter how savage their actions.

Finally they were subdued and Pedro walked over to Patten. His face was scratched. He smiled for the first time in the presence of Patten. He said, "Here are your banditos, Señor Patten. They are Yaquis. They have been left to die."

Patten nodded. He understood the custom. Looking at the wiggling pair, he concluded that death would not be long in arriving. The woman had begun to cough and was spitting blood. The child appeared to be about five years old. Her arms and legs were like broomsticks and her stomach was bloated. There was a white film over her eyes as if wrapped in layers of gauze, and it was obvious she was blind.

They carried them back to El Diablo, with the woman quiet and apparently resigned to her fate; the child sobbing wretchedly.

Among their laborers was a Mexican who spoke a smattering of Yaqui. He talked to the woman and attempted to ease her fears, but it was futile. She kept repeating *yori, yori* and this intensified the child's anguished cries. They refused food and Patten knew he would have two corpses on his hands unless he moved quickly.

The company plane had just returned from Durango. He decided to fly the pair to Zacatecas where Dr. Adams could treat them. It was the only humanitarian thing to do.

Once there, Dr. Adams diagnosed the woman's condition as tuberculosis and not likely to live beyond a few days. With the child, he had his doubts but he resolved to do what he could. He placed the woman in a hospital and took the child, her wrists still tied like a hostage, to his home, where they placed her in a guest bedroom.

When Carmen Adams first saw the emaciated child and heard her frantic jabberings she felt both pity and shame. How could this happen, she asked herself, even in the Sierra Madres? What kind of people would leave a blind child to die? Younger than her two brothers, Carmen had been born in San Antonio after her father and mother fled Mexico. She was completely anglicized and she longed to return to the United States, although this was a desire she shared with no one. Even in the city of Zacatecas, and although her mother had been a Mexican, she had found it hard to adjust to the quaint habits of the people and she had an instinctive fear of the brooding Indians who came into the city to market their crafts or barter gold and silver for merchandise. And yet now, staring at the trembling Indian child, she felt compassion. She had two children of her own. A girl, now a student at the University of Texas, and a son enrolled at the University of Mexico. She recalled their childhood years, so much in contrast to this piteous creature. She reached out and gently touched the child's matted hair, saying in Spanish, hoping she would understand, "I am going to help you. I will help you." As she spoke she unfastened the cord around the child's wrists. In retaliation, the child clawed her arm. Mrs. Adams jerked back in pain as the child wiggled into a corner and crouched with knotted fists like a defiant animal.

"Leave her alone," Dr. Adams said. "She'll calm down after awhile."

"The poor thing must be starved," Mrs. Adams said. She called to her maid, "Lucita, bring some milk and some bread and cheese."

When the tray was brought, Mrs. Adams advanced cautiously to the child, who was trembling now as perspiration trickled down her small face.

"Here," Mrs. Adams said. She placed the tray at her bare feet and said, "Drink the milk. It will make you feel better."

In retaliation, the child overturned the tray and flayed the air with her tiny fists.

To Lucita, Mrs. Adams said, "Bring another glass of milk."

The child refused the second glass and Mrs. Adams offered her a mango. "Here," she said. "It is good. It will make you feel better."

The child reached out and took the mango. She hurled it across the room, where it splattered against the wall.

"There's some *cabrito*," Lucita said. "That's what they mostly eat." She added disdainfully, "They let the goat meat hang from limbs of trees until it is dry and carry it with them in their wanderings. They know no better."

"Bring it," Mrs. Adams said. "Then we will leave her alone." Lucita glanced around the guest bedroom with its fine furnishings and embroidered spread. She sighed, "It will be a mess by then."

"We have no choice," Mrs. Adams replied.

When it was quiet, the child stretched out on the carpet and sobbed. She had clung like an embryo to her mother as if her umbilical cord had not been severed at birth. The warmth of her body, the stroke of her fingers and her words of affection had been all she had possessed. And now she was alone. Alone with serpents. Where was her mother? She asked herself. What had they done to her? Or, had she gone to the place in the sky? If so, why had she not taken her? She sobbed until there were no sobs left and dozed fitfully while absorbing strange sounds from outside the room. Sounds she could not identify, voices in an un-known language, an occasional honk of a horn which she interpreted as coming from birds of a kind she had never heard. Yes, she told herself when she awoke hungry and thirsty, she was in the land of the *yoris* and she was doomed.

She felt the tray and touched a strip of *cabrito*. Picking it up, she placed it against her nostrils and inhaled its familiar odor. Ravenously she ripped the meat with her fingers and chewed vigorously. When she had finished, she ran her hands over the carpet until she touched a glass. She smelled and then drank. It was goat's milk, sweet and rich and satisfying. When she finished, she lay down and slept.

Later, Mrs. Adams peered into the child's room and clucked her tongue sympathetically as she observed her on the floor. She was gratified that the meat and milk had been consumed. This was a first step, she told herself. She wondered if she should take the risk of placing her in the bed but decided it might awaken her. She was better left where she was and the thought brought sadness in the knowledge she probably had never slept in a bed. She placed a blanket over her. There was a placid look on the child's face now and Mrs. Adams studied it intently. Her bone structure was neatly fashioned to give her the look of an angel; and angel in need of nourishment.

The child's mother would not live long, her husband had informed her. Her tuberculosis was at an advanced stage. He was doing what he could but there was little anyone could do. Only a miracle could save her and as a medical doctor, he was not one to believe in miracles. That was for the priests.

"And what of her eyes?" she had asked him.

"It is more than a cataract condition," he said. "That is a disease in which the lens becomes opaque to cause partial or total blindness. It can result from many things during pregnancy. A common cause is the mother getting German measels during a certain period before the child is born. Yes, it is more than cataracts. Right now the need is to restore her to health. She would not have survived much longer in the mountains."

Mrs. Adams murmured a prayer as she stood over the child, then closed the door.

She awoke in the perennial darkness of her limited world at the sound of *yori* voices and feigned sleep.

Dr. Adams entered. He looked around and grimaced, "Well, first things first. I've got to give our little friend some shots."

"What kind?" Mrs. Adams asked.

"The usual innoculations plus vitamin injections. Lucita, do you think you can hold her?"

"Si, señor," Lucita said. She stooped and gripped the frail body in her sturdy arms as the child began to writhe and scream, certain now the *yoris* were going to kill her. She felt the prick of needles and interpreted them as the fangs of a serpent unleashing its poison into her body. When she was released, she backed away, still screaming, until she bumped against the wall. Ripping off her ragged garment she hurled it toward them before falling on the floor and pounding the carpet.

Mrs. Adams was in tears. She said, "It's not fair to do it this way. We've got to communicate. She's scared to death."

"I'm trying to save her from death," Dr. Adams rebuked her. "Señora Señora will be by in an hour or so."

"Who?"

Dr. Adams chuckled. "A character who speaks Yaqui."

Señora Señora had been brought unconscious into his company hospital suffering from injuries in an automobile accident about two years ago. Regaining consciousness, she had cursed him in several languages for his efforts but later a certain amount of respect developed between the two. She was of undefined race, although it was believed she was of gypsy blood. She had acquired a reputation in Zacatecas as a mystic and lived comfortably on pesos received from a loyal following. Señora Señora, this was her true name she insisted, had related some phases of her background, including her bizarre peyote experiences with the Yaquis.

Dr. Adams had visited her earlier in the day and she had agreed to talk to the child.

When she arrived, she was taken to the bedroom where the child was quivering on the carpet.

"Leave us alone," Señora Señora told them. Then she began speaking in Yaqui, "What is it, my child, that brings such torments from your heart and soul?"

The child considered this for a moment and asked, "Who are you?"

"One of you, one of everyone you have ever known. Are you afraid?"

"Yes."

"Why are you afraid?"

"They have taken my mother. They have let a serpent bite unto my body. I have been left alone to die."

"No one is alone. There are spirits everywhere," Señora Señora said kindly. "Can you not feel them?"

"I can feel *yori* spirits, nothing else."

"Have you felt the wind?"

"I cannot feel the wind here."

"No. This is because you are in a casa which locks the wind outside. But I ask you again, my child, have you felt the wind?"

"Yes."

"Does it sometimes feel cold and harsh?"

"Yes."

"This is the way with *yoris*, as with all tribes. Some are like a warm wind. Others are like a harsh wind in the winter when the snow is falling."

"All *yoris* are like the winter winds."

"No, my child, and I speak from many years of knowing. There are many *yoris* who are as warm as summer winds."

The child said defiantly, "I do not believe you. You lie."

"I do not lie," Señora Señora raised her voice. "Think now. Why would I lie to you? What would be my purpose?"

"I do not know," the child sobbed. "I want my mother."

"When were you last with your mother?" Señora Señora asked patiently.

"On the mesa."

"Why were you on the mesa?"

"We were left there," replied the child.

"Why were you left there?"

"To die."

"Why were you left there to die?" Señora Señora asked.

"Because my mother . . . she is sick. And . . . I am blind."

"Did your mother tell you she was sick? Did she tell you she was dying?"

"Yes."

"Did she say you were left there because you were blind?"

"Yes."

Señora Señora asked quietly, "Who left you there?"

"The others."

"The *yoris* did not leave you there?"

"No."

"It was others of your tribe?"

The child nodded.

"Then you cannot blame the *yoris*, can you?"

"No."

Señora Señora dipped into her purse and removed a bar of chocolate. She said, "Do you trust me?"

"I don't know."

"Would you trust me a little bit?"

"I guess so."

"I have brought you a gift. It is sweet like honey but of a kind you have never tasted. It is full of strength and this is what you need. Eat it and then we will talk some more."

The child reached out and Señora Señora handed the unwrapped bar to her. The woman sat patiently as the child sniffed, took a small bite and then devoured the bar.

"Did you enjoy it?" she asked.

"Yes. It was good."

"It is a gift from me, and from the *yoris*."

"Why would the *yoris* send a gift to me?"

"Because they want to help you."

"Where is my mother?"

"She is receiving herbs," the woman said, "But I speak the truth when I tell you it is likely she will die."

The child's blind eyes watered and she wailed, "Then I will die, too."

"No," Señora Señora said firmly. "You will not die. You are young. You have many happy years to live."

"I don't want to live!" the child shouted.

Señora Señora stood and shuffled her feet. She said quietly, "Are you sure you want to die?"

"Yes, yes!" came her defiant cry.

"No, my child. You want to live. Think now, do you really want to die?"

The child's voice came back doubtfully, "Yes."

"Very well, then," Señora Señora said. "I will leave. I will leave you with the spirits of death." She turned and moved heavily away, her sandals making a scraping sound.

"No, don't go," the child cried.

The woman took her in her arms and pressed her moist face against her bosom. "You must trust me," she said. "And I will teach you to trust others." She paused and stroked the child's matted hair. "Will you trust me?"

"I don't know."

"Will you try?"

There was long pause before the child said, "Yes."

"Good," Señora Señora said. "First, we must cleanse your body. Did your mother wash you in the stream?"

"I remember."

"Was the water cold?"

"I think so."

"The water is warm here and it is not a stream. It will make you feel better. Then we will clothe you with clean clothes and sit down together and eat a fine meal. Would you like to do that?

"I don't know."

Señora Señora took her hand and pulled her upright. "You must help a little bit, my child," she said. "If you want to live."

They entered the bathroom and Señora Señora placed her in a tub of warm water and bathed her body and washed her dark hair. As she did, she recounted fairy tales. She brought a first smile from the child when she told her the story of Cinderella and, when she had finished, the mystic felt a tingle. She paused in her scrubbing and looked at this skeletal figure with the face of a fragile madonna. Shaking her head in disbelief, Señora Señora helped the child from the tub and dried her body, thinking, is it possible, is it possible?

It was a gradual process, like restoring a scrubby plant to vigor or healing the broken wing of a frightened swallow. Señora Señora came whenever she could, but her time was limited. Dr. Adams was hard pressed with his professional duties and Mrs. Adams, a few weeks after the child's arrival, found it necessary to fly to the States when her daughter became ill.

The unnamed child, termed the "wild one" by Lucita, remained locked in the bedroom for fear she would attempt to flee. Also in the room were a pitcher of water and a wash basin. Food was provided thrice daily and the child learned to sleep beneath covers in the bed. She had not been told of her mother's death but after a few days she took it for granted that she would never see her again. Under instructions from Dr. Adams, Señora Señora taught her a few simple Spanish words and Yaqui gradually was eliminated. It was Dr. Adams' speculation she would never return to her tribe and should be made compatible with her new environment.

"Yesterday is over," he explained. "We're working for tomorrow."

"What about her eyes?" Mrs. Adams had persisted before her departure.

"I'll check that out later," replied Dr. Adams.

She was eating well now and her fear of the *yoris* had diminished, although there would be times when her defiance would return, especially when she was with Lucita, who resented her presence. The scant flesh on her body increased, as did her strength. With this came a desire to escape, to flee this narrow room and make it, somehow, back to her tribe. It was not far away, she reasoned. They had placed her with her mother in a strange whirling thing for a short time. She was probably only a short walk away from the mountains and they would accept her now. Or would they? she asked herself uneasily. She still was blind. If she returned, would they abandon her as before?

She missed her mother and at night she would snuggle a pillow and sometimes would hear her voice and feel her breath against her cheek as if she were with her. Sometimes she would have dreams, wild, frantic dreams; other times contented ones, and she often awakened to run her hands down the pillow hoping for a touch of her mother's body.

"She needs to be preoccupied," Dr. Adams told Lucita.

"We have a litter of puppies at our place," Lucita said.

"Good. Bring her one."

It was a mongrel, named Lobo, with a thick fur and a moist tongue and the child spent hours each day enjoying its company. She slept with it at night, despite Lucita's protests. At the same time, Dr. Adams brought the child toys, dolls that said "mama" and some that spoke in Spanish at the pull of a cord and more than anything, a tiny piano that tinkled when she touched the keys.

The sound fascinated her. It was like a voice from the past. She would lie on her stomach and press down on the keys with her head cocked as if in the mountains listening to chants.

When Mrs. Adams returned, she was delighted at the progress the child had made.

"She's almost doubled in weight," she told her husband. "There's no danger now, is there?"

"I don't think so."

"And no longer scared of us," Mrs. Adams said. "This was what bothered me. Trying to help and being feared."

"She's no longer afraid."

"Then don't you think we should let her have the roam of the house? I mean, keeping her locked in that room seems cruel."

"Whatever you wish," Dr. Adams replied.

Mrs. Adams let her explore her new environment. Their casa was luxurious by Mexican standards but not huge. It consisted of four bedrooms, two bathrooms, and living rooms, along with a patio of modest dimensions. In the parlor was a baby grand piano, which had come with their purchase, although it was seldom played. Mrs. Adams spent hours directing the child through the house and into the patio until it became familiar to her.

The child especially enjoyed the patio. She would run her long fingers through the grass and touch the flowers with a sense of well being. There were birds, too. And she would mimic them. Mrs. Adams brought her seed and it was not long before birds were feeding out of the child's hands.

One night, a month or so after Mrs. Adams' return, she awoke to the sound of music. It was a weird sound, or so it seemed as she awakened, and it was not coming from the street. It was from somewhere within the house. Hastily she moved from the bed and entered the studio room, where she paused in wonderment. The child was playing in the darkness. Her fingers were running over the keyboard with uncanny precision and from the piano came a barbaric tune which jangled her nerves. Mrs. Adams said nothing. Moments later, the child slipped from the stool and felt her way confidently to her bedroom.

"She has talent," she told her husband in the morning.

Her husband shrugged and said, "Talent is not restricted to any one race. In the isolated region of this country, or other countries, people of genius have been born and have died without acknowledgement." He smiled. "What if Shakespeare or Wagner had been born in the Sierra Madres?"

"But they were not," she said.

"Others were."

"You are saying that environment is essential?"

"Of course. A witch doctor is accepted only in a country which practices witchcraft. Put him in Kansas City and what have you got? It's the same with the creative arts. A writer has no outlet among people who do not read. Beethoven's great symphonies cannot be played without the proper musical instruments."

"And this wild child, as Lucita calls her?"

"She may have talent. We will find out soon, and, fortunately, she will be given every opportunity."

"We should give her a name."

"Yes. I have been thinking the same. Patten will be in town soon. I think he should be given the privilege of naming her."

Patten had been in the States and it was more than six months after the child's capture that he had time to visit Zacatecas and see her again. He was overwhelmed. "It's hard to believe," he told Dr. and Mrs. Adams. "She has a healthy look now and the fear seems to have left her. How did you do it?"

"A wise old woman who speaks Yaqui, nutritional foods and a big dose of love," Dr. Adams said. "Children thrive on love, you know."

They were talking in English in the patio as the child played with Lobo.

"She has exquisite features," Patten said. "Like a rose, a rose about to bloom."

"She needs a name," Mrs. Adams said. "What would you suggest?"

Patten let his gaze roam from the child to some rose bushes in bloom nearby. "Rosita," he said after a moment. "If that's all right with you."

They nodded their approval.

Rosita it was from that moment, instead of the "wild one" as Lucita has branded her, and "the child" as the Adams' had called her.

They sat at a table drinking coffee as Rosita gobbled ice cream with a contented expression on her face.

Patten, speaking in Spanish, asked her carefully, "Do you like it here, Rosita?"

The child cocked her head. He touched her arm and said, "Rosita. This is your name. It means a flower. A lovely flower called a rose."

The child shrugged, perplexed.

"She's made some progress but her vocabulary still is limited," Mrs. Adams pointed out. She walked over to a bush and snapped a rose from a branch. Placing it in the child's hand, she said, "Rose, Rosita."

The child felt the bloom and held it to her nostrils. She smiled.

"Rose, Rosita," Mrs. Adams repeated.

"Rose, Rosita," the child replied.

Later that day, they pondered her destiny. Mrs. Adams confessed she felt unqualified to raise a blind child with all the concentration it would entail, especially since she was suffering from angina and had to limit her activities.

"There's no rush, of course," she said. "Six months, even a year, but at my age and in my physical condition it would be better for Rosita, and for me, if she were placed with a family which could better meet her needs."

"I understand," Patten said. Turning to Dr. Adams he asked, "What about her eyes?"

"I have no idea," Dr. Adams admitted. "There are some excellent ophthalmologists in Mexico, particularly a Dr. Yves Elluard, whom I have met. He's a Frenchman with roots in Mexico dating back to the time Maximilian was emperor. How his ancestors survived the revolution would make a good story. Regardless, he's wealthy and one of the best eye surgeons in the world. I would recommend him although from what I understand he handles only a limited number of cases." He gestured with his hands. "Only the unusual ones, or among the aristocracy."

Patten jotted down his name and said, "I'll be in the city in a month or so. I'll give him a call." As he was speaking he gazed fondly toward Rosita, now curled on the grass in the warmth of the sun, sleeping peacefully as if without a care in the world. It was a touching scene and he vowed to do whatever he could to bring sight to her eyes.

Time slipped by for Patten. There were some business matters in the States and it was more than a month before he arrived in Mexico City. After a round of meetings, he placed a call for Dr. Elluard and was cordially informed that the surgeon was taking no additional patients. The receptionist gave him the names of three other ophthalmologists. Patten was a firm believer that first class was the only way to go. Instead of checking with the other doctors, he invited Juan Cepero to dinner and outlined his problem. Cepero was a prominent attorney with important political connections, and he knew Dr. Elluard. As a matter of fact, he said with a grin, he was his attorney.

Cepero arranged an appointment.

Dr. Elluard listened impassively as Patten told him the story of finding Rosita and her dying mother on the mesa near his mine and of taking the child to the home of Dr. Adams.

"She's a Yaqui, you say?" he interrupted at one point.

"That's what I understand."

"A noble tribe," Dr. Elluard said. "I have nothing but respect for them. And how old?"

"There's no way of knowing for sure, but I would say about six or seven."

"Healthy now?"

"It would seem. That's what Dr. Adams thinks and he's pretty professional on matters like that."

"Tamed, you say?"

Patten smiled. "The contrast is unbelievable."

Dr. Elluard looked quizically over his glasses into his eyes. "What is your interest in this?" he asked.

"I don't know for sure," Patten replied. "Except, somewhere along the way in life, after living in a competitive world which sometimes resembles a jungle, there comes a time when a man who has been comparatively successful feels a compulsive urge to help a victim of birth and environment."

Dr. Elluard said nothing. Instead he thumbed through his appointment book and then slammed it shut as if annoyed. Moving from his desk, he walked to the window and stared outside. It was a beautiful spring day and he looked down on a procession of pedestrians on the walks bordered by shops. Turning abruptly, he said tonelessly, "Zacatecas?"

"That's where she is right now."

"You have a plane?"

"Yes."

"Bring her in day after tomorrow at eight o'clock in the morning."

She awoke with a musty taste in her mouth and a desire for water and as she lay there she stretched her weak limbs and ran her hands over her face. Something was covering the upper part. It was hot and sticky and frightening. She lifted her head and groaned. Immediately there came a soft voice, "Do not worry, Rosita, do not worry."

It was Mrs. Adams. She had been at her bedside for hours and her prayers had been many. Dr. Elluard had been blunt in his analysis before the operation, saying in layman's language, "Her eyes are like an orange. Removing the peel is no problem but there's no way of knowing the quality of the fruit underneath."

The operation had taken more than two hours and Dr. Elluard had offered no optimism as he talked to Mrs. Adams in a tired voice for a brief moment afterwards.

Upon Rosita's awakening, they let her sip juice and she went back to sleep. She slept with tumultuous dreams and when she awoke someone was stripping the sticky binding from her face. There were no voices now. It was quiet, like the eye of a hurricane, as fingers and a cold cutting edge removed the bandages.

She opened her eyes and then blinked them shut as an intense beacon of light penetrated painfully into her pupils. She heard sounds, joyous sounds.

She remained in the hospital under sedation with specialists interrupting her sleep like phantoms in a procession. Finally she awoke clear-headed and looked around. She saw a world unknown to her and she screamed as if enduring a nightmare. Suddenly there were figures everywhere and assuring voices, "It's all right, Rosita . . . Don't worry . . . You can see!. . . ."

Rosita stared at the group surrounding her bed. What strange creatures, she thought. Was she one of them? Reaching out, she touched a face and felt a familiar outline of bone structure and a topping of hair. She raised her arm and wiggled her fingers in front of her face. These belonged to her, she realized. They were a part of her body. She had used them as long as she could remember and yet they looked funny. Smiling, she raised her head and stared beyond the people to notice objects she would later identify as chairs, flowers, drapes, windows, a door.

The voice of Mrs. Adams was close to her now and she stared at the face of the one who had been so kind to her. "Why are you crying?" she asked her.

"Because I am happy," Mrs. Adams said. She leaned forward and pressed her lips against her cheek. "So very,

very happy, Rosita." She stepped back at Dr. Elluard's urging. "You must sleep now, Rosita. We will be nearby."

"Learning to see after a life of blindness is not an easy task," Dr. Elluard explained to Mrs. Adams and Patten after they left the room. "Being young will make it easier, but don't press her too much. Sometimes she will close her eyes and feel with her hands as she has been doing. She may even be frightened by the sight of objects or people or animals. Does she have a pet, a dog or a cat?"

"A puppy."

"She may be startled by its looks, but not for long. Even with food. She has depended on smell and taste. Now she will see the ear of corn, the tortilla, the fish. And walking. She will stumble a bit at first because she has been walking in darkness." Patten started to speak but Dr. Elluard pressed on, "I know what you are about to ask, Señor Patten, and I can only say I think so. I believe her eyesight has been permanently restored, but I must keep her here for several more days and then schedule weekly appointments for an indefinite period."

A year went by and it was a remarkable one for the child, Rosita, with Dr. and Mrs. Adams and Patten enjoying her triumphant entry into her new world. Completely adjusted now, her body sturdy and her mind racing quickly like a fleet stag, she began to emerge as a young girl of strong personality and character.

Patten visited Zacatecas whenever he could. It was a gratifying experience for him, and, recalling her past, it seemed incomprehensible this was the waif he had captured on a mesa. Her skin was a light bronze and her cheekbones only slightly emphasized to give her the look more of a youngster of Castilian blood than that of an Indian. Her speech was precise Spanish with an abundance of English words gleaned from her environment. He felt a deep love for her and it was returned in abundance.

His was not the only love of Rosita. Dr. Elluard likewise had become infatuated with the youngster. Childless, the Elluards over the years had discussed adoption but had taken no action. The surgeon knew that Mrs. Adams was in failing health. Patten had confided it might be necessary to find a new home for Rosita.

At first the doctor had not even considered adopting her. There were several reasons for this. First, he would have preferred a male to bear his name; second, Rosita was of

Indian blood and he was familiar with the rigid customs of Mexican aristocracy. One day, as he was examining her, Dr. Elluard stepped back in surprise with the thought that this child closely resembled his godchild, Juanita, who had died at the age of six with her parents in a plane crash. It's incredible, he thought, incredible, and he attempted to dismiss the thought. The thought persisted uneasily in his mind.

He was on guard now; on guard against his growing affection, with the child unknowingly working her charms.

After a late afternoon examination, Dr. Elluard invited Patten to his home for dinner, where Señora Elluard first saw Rosita. The child was at her best, bubbling with laughter and skipping around the patio as if on wheels.

"You accomplished a miracle," Patten told the doctor, who replied, "The miracle was there long before I saw her."

After dinner, as the adults were talking, Rosita asked timidly if she could play the grand piano.

"Of course," Señora Elluard replied with interest. She asked Patten, "Has she been taking lessons?"

"Not to my knowledge. It's possible that Mrs. Adams taught her a few notes, but I think it's one of those natural talents."

"Talent?" Dr. Elluard asked.

"I don't know much about music, but it seems this way to me."

Rosita was playing now. It was a lyric of undefined title, jagged in spots but strong with barbaric intensity, and the child's small hands danced across the keyboard with brazen assurance.

They listened intently until Rosita wiggled from the stool and made a mock bow, her face solemn but with a beam of satisfaction in her lustrous eyes.

Señora Elluard said, "She does have talent; she is the right age, too. She should attend a conservatory."

Dr. Elluard nodded and turning toward his wife, asked, "Who does she remind you of?"

Señora Elluard studied the features of the child and gasped. "Juanita." She shook her head in wonderment. "It almost makes one believe in reincarnation."

Juanita had been the only child of Dr. Bernal Perez and his wife, Eleanor. Dr. Elluard had attended medical school at Harvard with Bernal and they had interned together at a general hospital in Boston before returning to Mexico. When Juanita was born, Dr. Elluard went through the ritual as godfather. The death of the couple and the child had been a hard blow. And now, she thought with a tremor, here was Juanita.

The visits continued over the months, with overnight stays at the Elluard home and one evening, over brandy and cigars, Dr. Elluard said to Patten, "I suppose you've noticed my affection for Rosita?"

Patten nodded.

"This is a captivating child and her mind is sharp as a whip."

Patten nodded again.

Dr. Elluard continued, "I understand Mrs. Adams' health is failing."

"Yes. Very much so."

Dr. Elluard said carefully, "Rosita has the look of a Spaniard more than an Indian."

"It seems that way to me."

"Fine features, aquiline nose, modest cheekbones, long tapered fingers."

"This is true," Patten said.

"As a matter of fact, she reminds me very much of the child of a friend of mine, a couple of the aristocracy who died in a plane crash along with their daughter."

"Oh?"

"Dr. and Mrs. Bernal Perez. You would have had no occasion to know them, but they were a family of distinction." He puffed at his cigar and said, "Much more acceptable than mine."

"Yours is quite acceptable."

"Yes, of course, but the Perez heritage dates back to Cortez. As a reward, the conquistador, Perez, was given large landholdings by the king." Dr. Elluard sighed. "If Rosita were a Perez she would be accepted anywhere in Mexico, or in Spain for that matter."

Patten was sensing his thoughts now. He asked, "The Perez family, the survivors, I mean. Is it a large family?"

"No. Its history has been one of tragedy. With the death of Bernal and his wife and child it has become extinct here in Mexico. There are some in the States and South America, I understand, but none here."

"And?"

Dr. Elluard moved his arm with cigar in hand and said: "You are more familiar with matters of this kind. To put it bluntly, if there were some way to record the birth of Rosita as the daughter of Bernal and Eleanor Perez it would be very much to her advantage in the years ahead."

"Yes . . . yes."

The two men sipped their brandy in the coolness of the evening and talked of other things. Finally Patten said, "The governor of Durango and I have become good friends. It will take time, of course, but he might be inclined to do me such a favor. I'll see him this week."

# 13

Time moved on. Rosita became the daughter of the late Dr. and Mrs. Bernal Perez and the adopted child of Dr. Yves and Danelle Elluard. The certificates had been filed and authenticated. The Indian child had become a member of Mexican aristocracy without knowing what had been done.

She was a happy child and she quickly adapted to the life of the Elluards from the time she arrived there at the age of seven. Her schooling was intense; a tutor in the home along with a governess, followed by a professor of music. She had become quite proficient as a pianist and she had a love for words. She spoke Spanish as well as French and English. Her young friends were those of the wealthy and Señora Elluard joined with other mothers in sponsoring garden parties, outings in the parks and an occasional flight to a beach resort.

Rosita had three major interests; horticulture, horseback riding and music. They constructed a greenhouse on their estate and she spent considerable time there. She was a natural rider, as her instructor said in admiration, and she would join others of her age, with chaperons, in traversing trails in the nearby mountains. Her ability as a pianist had progressed to the point where she was termed a virtuoso.

The past was dim now for Rosita. On one occasion, while riding with Dr. Elluard, she looked up at a towering peak and shuddered. He noticed and asked, "Is something the matter, Rosita?"

She ran her fingers through her hair and said, "Somewhere, somewhere, it seems something happened in the mountains. It frightens me."

"It's your imagination," Dr. Elluard asssured her. "A nightmare, perhaps. What is this something you are talking about?"

"I don't know," came her quavering voice. "It seems like . . . like I was alone up there, or alone with someone . . . my mother?. . . . I don't know."

"Dreams are such strange illusions," Dr. Elluard said quietly. "Some are good and others are bad. It is better to dismiss the bad ones. Come on, let's catch up with the others." He chuckled. "If not, there won't be any food left."

On another occasion, while visiting relatives of the Elluards in Curacio, she noticed some Yaqui braves in a store and heard their terse speech. Their words seemed familiar but she said nothing to her stepparents, thinking, it's foolish, stupid of me, how could I possibly understand their language?

She did remember blindness and the Elluards made no effort to conceal it from her, explaining she had been born with eye difficulties which had been cured by an operation. She let it go at that, although when she met a blind person she felt a fleeting kinship.

But these moods were secondary to those of maturing. She weathered these years while attending a private school for girls and complaining with the others of the restrictions. Upon graduation, she enrolled at the University of Mexico where there was more freedom, although Consuelo was lurking when she entered and left classes; a constant reminder she would not be a person in her own right until she married.

Rosita's meeting with Leon de la Cruz was through happenstance. He had just left the library, thinking of food and considering one of the many fine restaurants he frequented, when Rosita tripped on some books left on the steps and fell. He was the first to reach her. Helping her to her feet, he gazed with concern at her face racked by pain and said, "There's a bench over there. Can you make it or should I carry you?"

"My ankle," she said with a grimace.

He lifted her into his arms and placed her on the bench.

"Would you mind getting my books and purse," she said.

"I'll be right back."

"Not the ones I tripped on," she called. "Just two. Faulkner and Lewis." She made an effort to banter and added, "The others are dangerous."

What a strange combination, he thought, for he was familiar with both writers. As he found the books and her purse he remembered her now. She was Miss Mexico, having won the title last year, and she was in his biology class; shy and skittish like a young deer anticipating a hunter's stalk.

He placed the books and her purse between them and asked with genuine concern, "How's the ankle? I can take you to the hospital or to a doctor or to your casa. By the way, my name's Leon de la Cruz. You're in my biology class."

"I know," she said softly. "I've seen you."

"It's a large class," he teased her.

"I've seen you."

"And your name?"

"Rosita. Rosita Elluard."

"Your father's the surgeon? The ophthamologist?"

"I'm his adopted daughter."

"Dr. Elluard operated on my grandmother. Cataracts. She was well pleased."

"I'm glad."

"My car is not far from here. Can you make it? If not, I could carry you." He grinned. "You're not excessively heavy."

She massaged her ankle and smiled faintly. "In a minute or so I should be able to manage." Her large eyes, as magnificent as any he had seen, questioned him, "Are you late for a class? Am I intruding on your schedule?"

He reached over and touched her hand before quickly removing it. "You are not an intruder," he replied. "You are a welcome invader."

They sat silently for a moment before he tapped the books, and asked, "You have just checked these out?"

"Yes. For a paper in sociology." Her voice expressed interest. "Are you familiar with them?"

"Faulkner was a master but he must be read in English, otherwise the colloquialisms of his people just don't come through."

"This is in English," she said.

"And Lewis, in the other book, did a fine job in outlining the lives of an underprivileged family living here in Mexico City."

"There is much wealth and poverty here," she replied.

He nodded. "I am interested more in wealth than in poverty," he said, "But I do accept both. What is the theme of your paper?"

"To show that poverty, whether urban, as the Sanchez family in Lewis' book, or rural, as the Snopes in Faulkner's book, creates the same frustrating channels that lead to inertia and quite frequently degradation."

"It is a challenging theme," he said.

She removed her hand from her ankle. "I think I can make it now," she said. "If I can lean on you."

"It will be a pleasure, Rosita."

He helped her to her feet and placed his arm underneath her before asking anxiously, "Are you sure?"

"Is it far?"

"The red Jaguar over there."

She limped under his support to the car and he drove away.

Doctor Elluard was at home when they arrived. It was his habit to operate in the morning, preferably around eight o'clock, then attend to patients in his office until noon and forego afternoon chores unless emergencies developed. It was four o'clock now. He had eaten, taken a siesta, followed by a swim in the pool and was scanning a medical journal when the maid went to the door.

"Maria," said Rosita, "I've twisted my ankle. I hope that's all. Is papa here?"

"Oui mademoiselle," Maria replied in her awkward French accent.

Doctor Elluard tightened the belt around his trousers. He had been putting on weight and when he was at home he took certain liberties. He hastened toward Rosita and the handsome young man supporting her.

"Your ankle?" he asked.

"I stumbled, papa," Rosita said. "Outside the library. I don't think it's much." She turned her face toward Leon. "Papa, this is Leon de la Cruz."

"Yves Elluard," the doctor replied. "I am grateful, señor."

"Happy to do it."

The sprain was of minor consequence, Doctor Elluard determined, and he wondered if by some contrivance Rosita had concocted the fall to gain the attention of this young man with his continental manner and dress.

"It's not much," Dr. Elluard said. "Not even a need for x-rays although we'll take some tomorrow." He looked at Leon and asked, "Are you by chance from Durango?"

"I was born there. You saved the sight of my grandmother."

"Ah, yes. A charming lady. And your parents, too." Doctor Elluard knew of the vast wealth of the de la Cruz family and their son, standing before him, impressed him greatly. "You are a student at the university?"

"Yes sir," Leon said. He stepped back. "Is there anything I can do?"

"Nothing," Dr. Elluard said. "A pan of hot water with epsom salts should reduce the swelling." He smiled. "I'm quite sure she's not in danger."

Leon looked at Rosita and said, "It was a pleasure meeting you, although a painful one for you."

"The pain is of no consequence," Rosita replied. She followed him with her eyes as he left the casa.

Don Fernando de la Cruz and his wife were in the city a few weeks later and they paid a call on the Elluards. Don Fernando came quickly to the point, "My son, Leon, has mentioned your daughter, Rosita," he said.

"My adopted daughter," Dr. Elluard corrected him. "She is the daughter of Dr. Bernal and Eleanor Perez. They died in a plane crash fifteen years ago." He leaned back in his chair and went on, "I presume you are familiar with the Perez family. It dates back to the conquest of Mexico under Cortez. Diego Perez was one of the conqueror's captains. In reward for his services he received large landholdings in the State of Hidalgo.

Don Fernando's eyes softened. "Then he was a comrade of my ancestor, Captain Augustin de la Cruz, also with Cortez. It is coincidental to say the least."

"Bernal and I attended medical school and interned together," Dr. Elluard elaborated. "I loved him as a brother. With his tragic death, it seemed only proper for me to adopt his daughter."

"Yes . . . yes," Don Fernando said. "And Rosita, whom I have not had the pleasure of meeting, she was born here?"

"Another coincidence," Dr. Elluard said with a smile. "She was born in your city of Durango when Dr. Perez was doing research on some sort of bacteriological epidemic."

He shrugged as if it were a matter of little consequence and added tonelessly, "All the records are there."

Don Fernando nodded with equal nonchalance and said, "Our son, Leon, would like permission to pay his respects to your adopted daughter."

"I have met your son," Dr. Elluard said. "He is welcome in our home with Rosita's approval."

Thus began the romance of Leon de la Cruz and Rosita Elluard under the strict codes of Mexican nobility. They were never alone. Consuelo or a member of one of the families was with them every moment. The Elluards gave garden parties and they flew to Durango where lavish parties were held and they were part of a group attending the races at the world-famed Hippodrome race track in Mexico City, or riding in the mountains, or sitting opposite each other and talking quietly.

The courtship lasted a year and one evening Leon proposed marriage.

"Your parents?" she said.

"They have given approval. And yours?"

"Yes . . . yes."

"Then we will announce our engagement. There will be a wait, which I wish we could eliminate, but we have no choice."

"I regret the delay, too," she confessed. "But you are worth waiting for. I love you, Leon."

"You are the only one," Leon replied, and he took the liberty of pressing her hand against his lips under the scowl of Consuelo.

Now the waiting was over. The priest was concluding his marriage ritual in the cathedral in Durango and Rosita's heart was beating wildly. It had been almost two hours since the ceremony began and she was weary. How much longer would it last? She asked herself.

Leon was thinking the same. Getting married is more of an ordeal than getting born, he thought, with the memories of marriage firm in the mind instead of the bleakness of birth. He would steal a glance toward his bride and long for the moment they would be alone.

Finally it was over and he slipped a diamond and emerald ring on her trembling finger. They turned as the great organ of the church burst into triumphant music. Gripping each other's hands, they walked swiftly toward the door, their faces beaming.

Patten was staring in fascination. As the couple moved closely he caught the eyes of Rosita; eyes of ecstacy peering into his own with gratification, and he thought, looking at her regal appearance, Rosita, Rosita, misbegotten child left abandoned in the mountains, you have been born anew.


**The End**